EFFECTIVE NETWORKING FOR PROFESSIONAL SUCCESS

How to Make the Most of Your Personal Contacts

Rupert Hart

**KOGAN
PAGE**

YOURS TO HAVE AND TO HOLD
BUT NOT TO COPY

First published in 1996

Kogan Page Limited
120 Pentonville Road
London N1 9JN

British Library Cataloguing in Publication Data
A CIP record for this book is available from the British Library.

ISBN 0 7494 1597 5

Typeset by BookEns Ltd., Royston, Herts.
Printed in England by Clays Ltd, St Ives plc

Contents

Everybody knows there is no free lunch (so they'll
eat it anyway!) *27*; Contacting your friends *27*;
Summary *28*

Acknowledgements

Thanks to all my network partners and supporters: Hermione
Thompson, Torsten and Christine Hart, Tim Griffin and
Natalie Spiteri, Ronnie Ling, Jonathan Magin and Bea ten
Tusscher, Juliet Lecchini, Morgan Sheehy, Mike Woodhouse,
Rebecca Hind, John and Naomi Hanson, Michael Howell and
Karl van Horn, Mark and Anne Melling, Charlie and Elizabeth
Kenyon, Meli and Jean-Marie Gay, Neil Hart, Robin and Maria
Musgrove-Wethey, Alison Armistead, and not least, to my
father, Max (at last!).

CHAPTER 1

Why Networking Skills Are Critical for You

Have you ever seen a promotion you were the best for go to someone else? You had the better experience, the better knowledge, the better qualifications but it still went to someone else? Or, have you or your company pitched for a contract and lost to the chairman's friend?

If these or similar experiences have happened to you then you need to brush up your networking skills and this book is for you. Many people recognise the growing importance of networking and are looking for a more systematic way to approach it. If you always bear in mind that networking is, essentially, recognising and building on the power of shared experiences, then this book will add to that attitude the essential networking skills to make your professional life more successful.

Essential for both jobs and business contracts

With decreasing job security and the growth of small businesses, we are all 'self-employed' now. We are all selling something — our services or a product. So these networking skills are just as important for job-seekers, freelancers and small businesses.

The main skills covered here are finding contracts and work for your company, and finding a job. But the skills are applicable in all walks of life: from getting an article published, to finding someone who can supply a certain service, to winning money for charity work, to building a network marketing business.

Full of punchy action points proven in real life, it has short chapters so you can easily return to it and pick it up again. It addresses key concerns of overcoming inhibitors, and does not shirk from helping you to build the visibility you need.

Remember that when you are the best qualified person, you may deserve to get the job, but you won't win it without the essential skills of networking. It's no good waiting for your skills to be discovered: no one will see them and you will be passed over.

You've heard it before: 'It's not what you know, but who you know.' Now read on to discover the secrets of finding work (both jobs and contracts) effectively through recruiting able and willing 'network partners'.

Looking for business contracts

Networking is critical in the search for business contracts: not only for freelance contracts, but also for small businesses. With typically 30 per cent of the working population working for companies with fewer than nine employees, and with over 15 per cent self-employed in many countries, this skill is going to become even more critical for you in the future. It is in the small-business sector, particularly, that marketing is so important yet so difficult to do cost-effectively. Networking is the answer.

So you could advertise, couldn't you? Or have an entry in *Yellow Pages*? But these are becoming less and less effective, aren't they? Several trends are making these traditional routes to the decision-maker less effective:

- There are now so many publications and TV channels that you have to place many ads to reach enough people to make a difference. And the standard of the ads is such that you need to spend a large amount of money just to stand out from the 1,200 or so advertising messages we are bombarded with every day.

- As information about business increases, so competition gets hotter as companies reshape to match customer demands. That means cosy niches hidden away for a long time are now becoming illuminated and more companies are going for them. That makes it harder for you.
- Continuing layoffs and de-layering means that many people are setting themselves up as self-employed and competing on the same turf as you. So now there are more mouths wanting the same cake. That also makes it harder for you.
- As our economy moves much closer to a service economy, it is becoming increasingly harder to differentiate your services from everyone else's. Differences between companies' product offerings start to come down to intangibles like service with a smile, and reputations for reliability. And when there's nothing to choose on, they will choose on nothing. When words are cheap, it is hard to make the customer believe your words against your competitors'.
- People are much more aware of hype all around them. That means that, however heartfelt and factual your claims, people will be hard to persuade.

For all these reasons, you need to be cleverer than your competition. You need to think subtle and indirect. Working harder is no longer enough — you have to work *smarter*.

Networking is key for you in so many ways. You need information about what contracts are coming up before others do. You need to understand the key elements of the work because then it may be possible to help to write the conditions so that only you can meet all the needs. You need to build visibility with your target audience in order that you become seen as the natural choice for the work. And you need to be known by the decision-maker personally or through a personal connection so that he/she will know your reputation where skills are hard to measure.

Networking increases the odds of avoiding the costly competitive nature of pitching and winning contracts. It is, however, an art. This book makes it more into a science by systematising the process, while showing you how to make the process second nature.

Looking for a new job

On the job scene, networking is now becoming critical in gaining access to job opportunities and in appearing different from the other contenders for several reasons:

- Over 80 per cent of new jobs available are not advertised, being only posted internally, or filled by a friend of a friend. So for every job you see in the newspapers there are four times as many out there. That means that most people apply to the few ads there are and so the competition for these positions is fierce.
- Then advertisers are faced with too many applications for each job to cope with. They employ consultants to sift through the applications who screen them out using set criteria. The people who win these jobs, therefore, are people who fit the criteria exactly: so many years there, so many qualifications. This makes the answering-to-an-ad process useless for anyone who does not meet the criteria exactly.
- But how will the employer choose between people with the same credentials on paper? On something small, or inconsequential, and it is all down to chance: unless he knows the person!
- Several surveys have shown that, on average, the chances of getting a job through an ad in a professional or trade magazine or paper are below 7 per cent. Whereas getting a job through networking, by working out your skills, finding an employer who will value these skills, and arranging to see the person to hire these skills through your network partners can, if faithfully followed, achieve success rates up to 86 per cent. So networking can be up to 12 times more effective than merely answering an advertisement.

- You could apply to the company you want to work for directly. This is certainly a good strategy, and it is covered later, but you will have to try hard to differentiate yourself. In the late 1980s, an astounding 25 per cent of professional managers were laid off as companies de-layered. How will the employer tell you apart from everyone else? If you're a new graduate, you have even worse problems because you don't have the advantage of work experience to make you stand out. And the position's even worse if you're relatively unskilled.

You really need to have an inside edge about what the job is really about, what the employer's needs are, and how you can best fit the job. Even better if you can show that you are a nice reliable person who is fun to get on with. That's networking.

Overcoming natural inhibitions

The key problems most people face when thinking about networking are natural shyness, fear of being seen as 'using' people, and a fear of rejection. This book addresses these issues clearly and explicitly and will help you on them all.

- Networking is 'putting yourself about' to some extent and this does require some degree of 'outgoingness'. In the book we will show you how to learn these skills step by step until you are up there with the professionals. You don't have to glad-hand like a politician, nor change your personality to wear a star-spangled suit! Some of the best networkers are the most quiet mice. If they can be successful at it, you can too!
- Think of networking as something you have to do to get your rightful deserts, that everyone is doing it (except you), that it is now accepted practice, and that you are out to help people. Then you will start to overcome your fear of using people's connections.
- It can be painful to be rebuffed but when you realise that you are good, that you have successfully helped 'work-givers' in the past, and that (should they choose not to take

up your kind offer of your talents) they are not rejecting you personally, you will learn to overcome your fear of rejection.

Networking can be easy and fun. And you can get very good results with the minimum of effort if you know how and if you practise. So, while networking is never as easy as just sitting back waiting for the contracts or jobs to fall onto your lap, it needn't require more than a little concerted effort applied correctly.

Summary

- Networking is essential for both new jobs and business contracts.
- Effective networking can be 12 times more effective in getting a new job than answering advertisements.
- We are all 'self-employed' now.
- Advertising is becoming ineffective.
- Networking helps you to find hidden opportunities.
- Networking can help you to differentiate yourself from the competition.
- An indirect approach is needed.
- You can overcome your natural shyness, your fear of using people, and your fear of rejection.
- It's not difficult when you know how!

CHAPTER 2
The Three Key Networking Techniques

Now that you appreciate the need for networking skills and how very powerful they can be for you, you need to have a framework in which to put the action points of the following chapters.

Networking is all about using other people's interests and connections to differentiate you from the masses of competitors. This chapter will explain that networking consists of three interrelated techniques:

- hearing about opportunities from your 'network partners';
- reaching targeted individuals; and
- building visibility.

If you like, you can think of networking as self-marketing with you and your skills as the product. You need to do market research on your customers' needs, engage in direct marketing, and raise your profile through subtle public relations.

Don't skip through this chapter quickly: you will find it very useful as you pull all the individual steps together to implement your 'campaign'.

Hearing about opportunities from your network partners

In the Vietnam War the US forces placed sophisticated listening microphones along the Ho Chi Minh trail. These devices radioed back when people were walking along the path. You need to think of your network partners as advanced listening posts, or scouts.

This is what people usually mean when they say 'networking'. And it is this more than anything which has become so important, now that so many contracts and jobs remain hidden from the written word.

Reaching targeted individuals

This technique can be likened to a guided missile which crosses difficult terrain to get to the target. Or, perhaps better, as a pinball which bounces off several barriers (which are your network partners) before hitting the jackpot.

Once you have identified which company is likely to be a good source of work, and found the likely decision-maker, understood his/her likely needs, and worked out how you are going to position yourself against the competition to meet his/her needs better, then you need to reach that decision-maker.

The book describes two methods of reaching targeted individuals:

● through your network partners; and
● directly.

The indirect approach, through your network partners, works by exploiting connections and areas of common interest to get past the secretary and into the willing ear of the decision-maker. The direct approach is less effective in general and works by sending a letter and/or making a phone call.

Building visibility

Networking by building visibility is rather like a woman or man walking through a crowded party after putting on a subtle perfume or after-shave respectively. It is not a process which will immediately yield results and can be difficult to control but is a powerful way of raising your profile. In general, this third networking technique can take longer than other methods but that should spur you on to begin today, as the following story demonstrates:

One of Napoleon's marshals was sitting in his garden one day when his gardener came up to him.

'Marshal, what would you like me to plant in that corner, there?'

The marshal replied that he should plant a certain tree.

'But, Marshal', the gardener exclaimed, 'that tree takes a century to mature!'

'Better start now, then', exclaimed the marshal.

In the real world, advertising is becoming less effective, and public relations (PR) more important and cost-effective. The process of finding contracts and jobs is beginning to follow this trend, and networking by building visibility has many parallels with PR.

Let us explore this analogy a little further. What is PR and how is it different from advertising? When an editor writes in a newspaper and mentions that he really liked test-driving a certain car, this will induce a positive feeling in readers towards that car. This exposure has not cost the manufacturer more than a few gin and tonics and maybe the use of a car for a while. Since the editor is considered by the public to gain no benefit from giving this opinion, they will place much more trust in his opinion than they will on advertising by the company. In the same way networking by building visibility can appear to involve less effort, carries more weight because it is a referral, and is inexpensive.

You can raise your profile subtly by a variety of approaches and then later your name will naturally come to mind and people will start talking of you in hushed tones. The snowball will start rolling and the work flow will increase.

Deciding which approach to use when

Each of these three approaches has advantages and disadvantages. In the next chapter we will begin to plan our campaign and so we will need to understand which technique to use for which purpose. In the table below the networking technique of reaching targeted individuals has been split into direct and indirect to show the differences more clearly. The assessments of each method's efficiency are necessarily subjective but should help you to choose the right approach for your situation.

	Network partners hearing about work opportunities	Reaching targeted individuals directly yourself	Reaching targeted individuals indirectly through network partners	Building visibility
Do on your own?	No	Yes	No	No
Short or long term?	Medium	Short	Medium	Longer
Effective?	Moderate	Moderate/Low	Extremely	Very
Requires much effort?	Moderate	Low	Moderate	Moderate
Overall efficiency	Better	Good	Best	Better

It becomes clear that while all methods, if properly applied systematically as outlined in this book, will give you good results, some techniques will give you a much better return on your efforts and should be given higher priority. In general, the best approach tends to be that of narrowing down the area of focus of your search and then using your network partners to reach your target decision-maker indirectly.

The structure of this book

This book concentrates on achieving results quickly. This immediate emphasis will mean relying initially on your existing range of contacts. You are therefore recommended to apply the three key networking techniques to your present network, while developing your contact base in parallel. The structure of the book reflects this process by discussing the important methods in turn, interspersed with motivating chapters to help you overcome your inhibitors.

It is strongly recommended that you read the chapter headings again to understand the contents of the book, and to read through the book quickly first so that you can better understand how a combination of approaches will maximise your networking efficiency.

Summary

There are three techniques involved in networking.

- Build a network of network partners to hear about opportunities for you.
- Reach targeted individuals in two ways: directly or indirectly.
- Build visibility to raise your profile.

In general, the best way to network is to reach targeted individuals indirectly through your network partners.

As an ongoing process you need to constantly increase your range of contacts.

CHAPTER 3
Plan Your Campaign

As in all activities in life, you need to sort out your objectives and plan to get the greatest possible effect from the least possible effort.

If you talk to anybody who's gone through the networking process for the first time, they always say that when they look back on their endeavour, only a small fraction was of real benefit in achieving their objective, and that if they had been focused from the start they would have avoided so much wasted exertion. This chapter will help you do the same.

The planning process

Follow the process shown in Figure 3.1 to make best use of your time.

Define your objective

It is all too easy to be distracted by opportunities which come your way and are not close to your objective. This is often a problem at the beginning of the process because the inevitable delay between effort and result means there are few opportunities arriving at first and we can be tempted to jump at every opening. But the good possibilities take time to unearth themselves and if you spend too much time on options which are not taking you in the right direction you

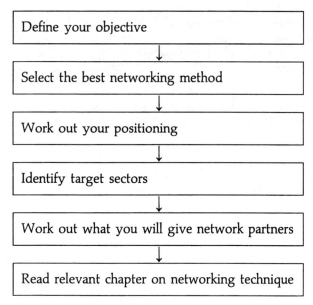

Figure 3.1 *Step-by-step planning*

will waste time you could have spent on searching. So write down briefly in one line what your priorities are and what your ideal is. Then when an opportunity comes by you can check whether it is right for you.

Select the right networking methods for you

You need to select the networking method which meets your needs. Two key questions you need to have clear in your mind are:

- Can you afford to take your time to find the right opportunity?
- How well can you target the companies you want to reach?

There is a trade-off: the more urgent your needs, the lower your standards are likely to have to be, since the better opportunities tend to be less obvious, more competed for, and thus require more networking skills to persuade the decision-maker. For example, going direct to a decision-maker yourself will not be as powerful as going through a mutual contact because the decision-maker may be bombarded with many such approaches and cannot differentiate yours from everyone else's. Developing mutual network partners takes time but will be a great deal more effective.

If you can define your objective closely enough, if your skills or product really can meet the needs of your target customers/employers, and if there are enough targets available, then you should go for a targeted approach to reduce effort wherever possible.

Since there is always an element of luck in these things, you are recommended to use several approaches at once, but prioritise the one approach that best seems to meet your needs. You may find that your target area is not as 'target-rich' as you first thought. You may find that your targets are not responding as favourably or as quickly as you expect and that you will have to wait longer. In these cases you will be glad that you warmed up your network partners to look for opportunities, and built visibility.

Why 'deal-flow' is so critical

In planning your campaign, be sure you understand that you do need a large number of prospects coming past your door all the time to have a reasonable number coming inside. You can't just sit back and wait for the phone to ring, and for the 'bluebirds' to land on your windowsill.

Finding opportunities for contracts and jobs of the right sort is rather like pouring water into a series of weirs. Each reservoir can be thought of as a stage in the process, from investigating options to the final stage of finding an opportunity. Like an interconnected water system, it starts empty, and needs to be primed. This is done by continually pouring in possibilities at the top. To achieve an even flow out at the end requires constant topping-up. And there is a time lag between beginning to fill the system and something coming out at the bottom.

Identify target areas of opportunity

If you are not to be buffeted by storms of unpredictable opportunities all requiring thought to work out if they are useful to you, and to avoid wasted effort, you should define your target sectors of opportunity.

Start with all the sectors you have already worked in. Now ask yourself what key skills you developed and where else those skills could be used. Brainstorm with friends or colleagues.

Another way is to look at people doing the same thing as you. To whom else do they sell their services? Could you do the same?

If there is a gap between what you do and what you would like to do, can you add capability by additional training or buying in outside expertise or products?

At the end of this you should come up with a list of sectors that could use your expertise. Then prioritise them so that you identify your top three.

Work out your positioning

Positioning is a marketing term and means a crisp one-line statement of what makes you and your services or product special.

And special means different from the competition in a way that's meaningful to the 'customer' – be it a buyer or an employer. Let's concentrate on the three words of 'meaningful', 'competition' and 'different'.

Meaningful
Work out what is really important for your customer. If, for example, he wants a person for a task, what three key points would be emphasised in a job advertisement? These are the three key criteria that the employer will select on. Anyone who doesn't meet them will be screened out. Then think about what other factors may be important for him. Overall, these qualities of the individual are what are meaningful to the

21

customer. Therefore what you have to offer needs to be pitched to show the customer you have understood his needs and that you can meet the most important ones. The same principles apply whatever you are selling: your skills and time, your company's skills and time, or a product.

Competition

Think of the 'customer's' alternatives: either people or companies similar to you or wider alternative sources. For instance, if your company is a supplier of garden furniture, the buyer could buy from:

- you;
- another garden furniture supplier;
- an auction;
- a second-hand shop; or
- he could borrow furniture; or
- hire premises with furniture already supplied.

Sometimes the 'customer' may not know that he needs someone or something. Therefore the alternatives will be much wider for him. So try to understand what the 'customer's' alternatives are and then figure out how you are better.

Different

For different, read better. And this means demonstrably better. How are you going to prove your claims? Here are some suggestions:

- awards, results of tests, qualifications, prizes;
- customer or employer references;
- list of significant achievements (and how you could do the same for them); and
- show that you have identified their problems and suggest solutions, so demonstrating an in-depth knowledge.

When putting together your CV or your sales brochure, it often helps to go through all the papers and historical records you have to bring all your achievements to the surface.

Now see if you can put it all together. Knowing your target market and their needs, and knowing how you can meet them better than the competition, write a three-line summary of yourself, your company or its product offerings. This will be your positioning statement or your calling card. This is what you want them to remember about you, This is your guide when you meet an opportunity out of the blue and do not know whether to go with it or not.

Work out what you can contribute when you make contact

You need to have an idea about what you can offer a contact to make it worth his or her while to look out for opportunities for you, to introduce you to decision-makers, and to help build visibility. Start thinking about these aspects now. We will come back to this area later on in more detail.

Summary

- Understand the importance of planning in making networking effective.
- Define your objective.
- Select the right networking technique.
- Understand why 'deal-flow' is so critical.
- Identify your target sectors.
- Work out your positioning.
- Start thinking about what you can offer your network partners.

CHAPTER 4

Overcome Your Fear of 'Using' People

You probably have a psychological block on the whole idea of networking. Maybe you feel it's 'Machiavellian' or somehow underhand. This isn't really so if you approach networking the right way. And the whole concept will become second nature to you after a while.

Networking is morally right, eases some of the inefficiencies in the business world, and, most importantly, is of great use to the 'work-giver' in bringing your products and services to his attention. Your network partner feels you are providing a service which makes it worth his or her while to help you along.

After reading this chapter you will know for sure that you can engage in networking without guilt, provided you are willing to put into it as much as you take out of it.

You scratch my back, and I'll scratch yours

If you feel guilty that you are exploiting or 'using' your network partners then you are not providing or planning to provide enough in return for their help.

The nature of networking is such that your contact will not help you indefinitely out of altruism. He expects something in return: at the very least thanks and respect now, maybe

Figure 4.1 *'You scratch my back ...'*

information or some other favour from you in the future. In a way, networking is a mutual help society which replaces the extended family structure of former days where each family member would help everyone else.

If you are genuinely willing to ensure that your network partners get more out of their association with you than they have to put in, then you will network successfully. If you do favours for people, moreover, you will develop a reputation for helpfulness which will encourage people to help you.

It isn't something just for 'yuppies'

You may be feeling that only young upwardly mobile people 'on the make' would engage in such a systematic way of getting to know people. If so, you'd be wrong.

Everybody networks to some extent. For example, the gardener keeps his gardens tidy, says hello and has a chat with his boss, and offers planting tips to strangers in the bar. All of which gains him continued employment with his employer and earns him part-time cash from tending others' lawns.

Until you become a 'natural', you will have to follow the systematic way in this book. After that, you will be following it naturally without realising!

Everybody's doing it: an accepted practice

More and more people are becoming aware of the need for networking just to maintain their positions and hang on to their existing contracts, let alone win new business. The fact that you are reading this indicates that you appreciate its importance and that everyone is doing it.

If you don't learn how to network you will be left behind. Your skills and abilities will be overlooked and lesser people will take the rewards you deserve because they are applying these networking skills. Don't let it happen to you!

Be genuine in your desire to help while networking

They say you can't buy friendship, that it has to be earned. The key to really successful networking is to make it so much a part of your life that it becomes an essential life-skill which helps all around you.

We can all learn from former US President Lyndon Johnson, an inveterate networker, who had these rules taped to his desk:

- Learn to remember names. Inefficiency at this point may indicate that your interest is not sufficiently outgoing.
- Be a comfortable person so there is no strain in being with you. Be an old shoe, old hat kind of individual.
- Acquire the quality of relaxed easy-going so that things do not ruffle you.

- Don't be egotistical. Guard against the impression that you know it all.
- Cultivate the quality of being interesting so people will get something of value from their association with you.
- Study to get the 'scratchy' elements out of your personality, even those of which you may be unconscious.
- Sincerely attempt to heal, on an honest Christian basis, every misunderstanding you have had or now have. Drain off your grievances.
- Practise liking people until you learn to do so genuinely.
- Never miss an opportunity to say a word of congratulation upon anyone's achievement, or express sympathy in sorrow or disappointment.
- Give spiritual strength to people, and they will give genuine affection to you.

Everybody knows there is no free lunch (so they'll eat it anyway!)

When you take somebody out for lunch, the other party has a good idea that you want something. But that's OK: you are giving something in return for their time and they expect to get something out of it, too. So there is no need to feel guilty.

Contacting your friends

Many people feel there are special problems when contacting their friends. Let us examine some of the fears you might have about phoning up a friend.

'I don't want to impose on them'
If you are especially above board with explaining why you are contacting them, they will understand. So long as you are careful in your wording (and your intentions) you should not make them feel uncomfortable. Don't make them feel obliged. Use phrases like these:

- *'If you happen to come across something like this, let me know, won't you?'*
- *'I need your brain for a moment. I need some creative ideas to solve this problem.'*
- *'You're the most well-connected person I know.'*
- *'Fred recommended that you might be able to suggest ...'*

'I am risking my friendship by asking for help'
If you think clearly about this, you will see that this should not be the case. Everybody likes to be helpful, if they can. But if you ask them to do something which will make them uncomfortable without leaving them an escape route, or something risky, then you could very well risk a friendship. So the secret is never to push too hard, and to back off when things get difficult. Learn to be sensitive to the other's voice and body language.

- *'I would really appreciate a moment of your time.'*
- *'I could really use some help. Can you help me?'*

Summary

- People will help you if you help them.
- The power of networking is becoming widely recognised.
- Learn to network or lose out to those who do.
- Really want to help others as they help you.
- Be a comfortable 'old hat, old shoe' kind of person.
- If you help someone, they know they should reciprocate.
- Your friends won't be offended if you ask them for help.

CHAPTER 5

Hear About Opportunities from Your Network Partners

The first key networking strategy is to gather information regularly on the latest opportunities. This chapter will show you how to maximise the number of opportunities presented to you and make sure that they are the right sort for you to take advantage of.

Think of this chapter as showing you how to listen out for opportunities in two ways: first, by yourself talking to your existing range of contacts, and second, by putting out scouts who will continue to look out for breaks for you. These could be people you know well, are nearer your areas of interest, or people who are particularly well connected.

Ask everyone you know, and everyone you meet

Most people are amazed at the vast range of potential sources of information they already possess in their existing network. As we will see throughout the book, opportunities originate from strange quarters, often the least expected. So get yourself swimming in these information flows. Check out the list given below for some suggestions and remember to talk to everyone you meet as well, not just the people you know!

- family – near and extended
- friends – your own, family friends, the parents of your children's friends
- colleagues at work and former colleagues
- parent–teacher association
- church
- bank
- hairdresser or barber
- insurance broker
- taxi driver
- participants on training courses
- customers
- suppliers
- shop assistants
- people met on holiday
- people sitting next to you on the plane, train or in buses
- members of sports clubs
- associations, charity organisations.
- political organisations
- local or parish council
- (fellow prisoners!)

The function of network partners

It is not enough to have contacts, you really need to have network partners: people who are partners in your quest, people who will do things actively on your behalf. They are motivated *by you* to search for opportunities *for you* and pass back information on them *to you*. And, if they meet a decision-maker or a contact, will put forward your name to them.

Which contacts to build into your network partners

Given unlimited time, you will want to make everybody a network partner. However, we suggest that you focus your efforts at least initially on those people who:

- respect you;

- like and understand you; and
- are in areas relevant to your objective.

Remember that people do have unusual connections across many industries, countries and groups of friends and so your efforts should not be restricted to the people suggested above. Wherever possible spread the word and recruit network partners whenever you meet them.

Find the friendly 'network spiders'

It is amazing, isn't it? The way some people just seem to know everybody, or have some connection with virtually anybody you mention. Chances are, these people are 'network spiders': people who are genuinely gregarious, interested in people, often older, and superlative networkers on their own account. Like spiders they are in the middle of a web and are sensitive to the vibrations caused by 'opportunities' from even far away. Look around you: who are the 'people who know people'?

These are some of the most powerful levers of your campaign to network your way to a new contract or a new job. You can charm them into helping you for, even if they do not know of someone directly who can help you, they know someone who knows someone who might!

So how do you find these people? Here are a few suggestions:

From among your personal friends
- Which of your friends is usually the centre of attention?
- Who is the person you most admire for knowing everybody?
- Who always seems to get the juiciest jobs?
- Who always knows where you can get hold of something?

From the industry
- Who is the most well-known person in the industry?
- Who is in a position to oversee the whole industry (a trade association president, editor or journalist, a head-hunter or a recruitment consultant)?

How to get in touch with your contacts

There is no question that the telephone is the best way to reach any of these people. It has several key advantages:

- It gets results quickly.
- It brings a degree of informality and openness that a letter cannot.
- It involves the contact in only a minimum of inconvenience (no need for them to write a letter to you).
- It allows feedback on the contact's disposition which allows you to customise your approach during the conversation and provide information to your contact.

How to build contacts into your network partners

The key is to motivate them and make sure they are fully briefed about your skills and needs.

The motives for your personal network partners might be that:

- they would like to see you happy;
- they enjoy helping people;
- they enjoy receiving thanks;
- they expect you to help them in the future;
- you're a nice person and they enjoy your company.

What to tell them about yourself

What do you tell them? In essence you need to give them the following information:

- why you are calling them;
- what you are looking for (information, contract opportunities, job vacancies);
- how you are positioning yourself against the competition; and
- some of your relevant achievements.

We go through the finer details of the conversations in a moment but remember to:

- warm them up with social conversation if possible;
- mention any name who referred you to them;
- bring up any connection you might have with them.

When you place that call don't forget the tried and tested method of adding stature to your voice, relieving your nervousness, and putting the other person in a good frame of mind towards you:

- stand up as if you were in the same room; and
- smile and gesticulate (the smile really transmits down the line!).

You may find the more detailed list of suggestions for talking to the decision-maker himself (see Chapter 10) also applicable here when talking to potential network partners.

Putting all the techniques into practice can have your network partners really working for you, as you can see in the following real-life case study:

Case study: a true story about getting a job through networking

Jonathan was focused on a job in marketing in Eastern Europe. In addition to direct written searches and letters to companies, he phoned up 10–15 people he had met professionally from several years before. These were mainly accountants and lawyers he had dealt with in previous companies he had worked for. He explained that he was looking for leads for a job in this area and could they meet for a chat. In most cases they were able to find time to meet. One person took Jonathan to lunch and gave Jonathan five more names to call. Jonathan rang all five and got through to the contact using the name of the network partner. They were all very helpful.

One put him in touch with a friendly 'network spider' at the Department of Trade and Industry in charge of helping British companies in Eastern Europe. That lady then kindly sent a list of exporting companies to Jonathan, saying that she was

---

happy for him to use her name, and he then proceeded to contact them all systematically.

Meanwhile, one of those companies telephoned the lady at the DTI saying they were looking for someone for the Eastern Europe area: did she know of anyone? She did and was able to pass on Jonathan's details. That company telephoned Jonathan.

Today Jonathan is proud to be the Marketing Manager for that company's Eastern European operations.

Summary

- Talk to everyone you know and meet about opportunities.
- Understand what network partners can really do for you.
- Understand which contacts to build into network partners.
- Find friendly network spiders.
- Use the telephone.
- Build contacts into network partners.
- Make sure they know about you.

CHAPTER 6

Grow and Refresh Your Existing Network

We have so far been focused on achieving results — whether a contract or a new job — quickly, using your existing range of contacts. We now deal with the longer-term but essential task of growing and refreshing your network.

Think of this not as a task but as an interesting opportunity to learn more about people, to help them in return, and to tell them what you are doing with the help they have given you.

This chapter will help you to generate more contacts and turn more of them into proactive network partners. We start with growing the network and then move on to refreshing your existing contacts.

Grow your network

There are three steps to expanding your range of contacts:

1. Go out of your way to be where people are.
2. Get into the habit of being talkative with people you meet.
3. Get the contact details of the people you meet.

Go out of your way to be where people are

Think of all the gatherings there are and push yourself to go to them to meet people. It is fun when you treat it as an adventure. And when you realise your future is at stake, you will force yourself into the cold at the end of a long day to network with people who may help you to build your future the way you want it to be.

Here are some suggestions. Even the most unlikely meetings can lead to meeting someone interesting.

- trade association meetings
- conferences and training courses
- exhibitions and trade shows
- office parties
- funerals
- sports clubs
- social clubs
- church
- the Freemasons
- charity associations
- pubs
- parties of friends of friends

You are very strongly advised not to miss your office Christmas party under any circumstances.

Get into the habit of being talkative with people you meet
Clearly, there is little point going to a gathering and eating peanuts around the fringes. You need to talk to people to discover information about them (and later how you can be of use to each other). A conversation is a discussion of common interests and therefore the start of a conversation is usually based on something you have in common with the other, and then you move on to other areas of mutual interest, usually enjoyed with a sprinkling of humour or with a similar style.

There are, therefore, three important elements of being talkative:

1. Establish common interests and connections.
2. Have something to say on every subject.
3. Adopt a likeable style.

Establishing common interests requires you to ask questions, listen actively, enjoy the banter of conversation and to have an interest in the person as a human being. Getting a conversation started and working out whether the other is receptive can require practice at first: find anything in common as an entry:

- the weather
- the suit/dress/ watch/ jewellery they are wearing
- whom they know at the gathering
- where they have come from today
- what they are here for
- where they are spending their next holiday
- how long they have known the host
- how they met the host originally
- who else they know and how they met.

Sometimes at a party you will meet someone who is interested in only one thing and it isn't one of your interests at all. To you he will therefore be boring. Without realising it, you may be seen as boring by some people because you have an obsession or because you have a very narrow range of interests. Take a look at yourself. Chances are you will have to develop more interests. Here are some suggestions:

- Take up a new sport or watch one.
- Try a new hobby.
- Read a newspaper every day.
- Watch TV programmes.
- Visit new places (the next pub, the next town, another country).
- Do new things.
- Read widely (human interest, current affairs, the Royal family, *Readers Digest*, humour).
- Play a new game.
- Go to exhibitions, shows, galleries.

In short, develop many and varied interests. Once you have found out what excites your new contact you can tell them a story about an aspect of their interest. Learn how to tell stories so they entertain and you do not feel embarrassed. Never impose your point of view: ending with a question is always a good idea. And don't forget to allow the other plenty of time to speak.

If there is a quiet spot in a conversation you feel uncomfortable with, ask another question.

Get the contact details of the people you meet

If you find someone who is interesting, whom you like (and who likes you), and especially if you have something specific in common, make a point of swapping contact details so that you can reach them later.

If this feels uncomfortable, try offering your card to them. They will almost certainly reciprocate with theirs. If you don't have a business card, or it is not appropriate, why not have a personal card made?

If you really feel that it would not be right to ask for a name, address and telephone number, then afterwards make a note of their name, any details, and how you might reach them again (their company, whom they know and through whom you could reach him or her).

Remember not to stop the conversation once you have their contact details: they do not want to be thought of as just another contact! Also, it can be a good idea to arrange to meet them again before you say goodbye. As explained in Chapter 14, you should drop them a note on some pretext the next day so that you remain memorable.

Refresh your network

The key is always to remain in 'front of mind' so that these network partners will make a connection between opportunities that pass them and your needs. This means frequent and customised contact. Here are a few suggestions for keeping in touch regularly:

- Send any articles or snippets of information you hear about which you feel would be of interest to your network partner.

- Send an annual review of how the last year has treated you.
- Send Christmas cards (very important).
- Phone them up on St Patrick's Day (if they're Irish).
- Phone them up on their birthday (or children's birthdays).
- Phone up your contacts regularly: three every Sunday night.

You may not be able to find time, or it may not be worth your while contacting some of your network partners as often as others. Therefore you will have to customise your approach to each person. Be careful, too, of over-communicating to some people who would be irked by this.

Warm up long-cold contacts

This is perhaps the trickiest effort at first sight, but needn't be. A good start would be sending a letter or a Christmas card. Here say you are sorry that you haven't been in touch lately, and that you would like to meet or hear about their news. Use lots of questions to show your interest. Mention any mutual acquaintances to tease them to talk to you. Then offer to contact them in the near future so that they do not have to do very much. Don't let them get cold again!

It is not recommended that you mention any specific need in your letter (ie new job, more work) so that they do not feel under obligation. This is best mentioned offhand at the end of your telephone conversation, or sometime when the other asks you about your life at the moment.

Summary

- Go out of your way to be where people are.
- Get into the habit of being talkative.
- Get the contact details of the people you meet.
- Choose the right contact method for each person.
- Warm up long-cold contacts.

CHAPTER 7
How to Find Targeted Individuals

Of the three key networking techniques, specifically targeting an individual is the most efficient. We then have a choice of a direct approach to that person, or an indirect approach using network partners to introduce you to them. These can be some of the fastest and most cost-effective approaches but require some unusual detective skills on your part.

This chapter concentrates on finding the key decision-maker, or 'work-giver'.

Be very focused

You will use a lot less energy if you are focused in your aim and head directly to where you want to go. Work out exactly which company to approach, who the key person is, what his or her needs are and how you can meet them better than the competition, and, most importantly, how you are going to get the 'work-giver' to listen to you in the first place.

Unfortunately, just telephoning that person and asking for a contract or job is often less effective. So we need to edge our way towards that person like a tiger in the jungle, getting close using our camouflage.

The first step, then, is to work out on which companies to focus our efforts.

Find the company

There are two ways of finding the names of companies — through written sources and through your network partners.

Assuming you have read Chapter 4 and have asked your friends and network partners for names of companies they feel you could successfully work for, you now have to use written information sources to ensure you have enough names, and to refine the list of companies you already have.

First, ask yourself what information you need to know. Here are a few suggestions:

- What companies are operating in the sector?
- Which are big enough to hire my services?
- Which are in my area?
- Which are reputable companies?
- What market shares do they have?
- What products and services do they sell (names, specifications, differences from competition)?

Your public library or local business reference library should have what you need. Other alternatives are careers guidance centres and trade associations.

Where can you find out this information from written sources? Try the following:

- directories of business services (*Kompass*, etc);
- *Yellow Pages* in your area;
- the trade association (see a directory of trade associations);
- list of members of a trade association;
- company accounts;
- product literature and brochures from the company;
- the list of advertisers in specialist magazines;
- list of conference attendees;
- list of exhibition participants;
- *Financial Times* survey of the industry;
- market-research reports (available for free inspection at certain specialist public libraries);
- press database searches for references and articles about the company.

Find the person with the power to hire you and your services

In order not to waste your efforts you need to understand who the key decision-maker is for your services and what the decision-making process in the company is. You should feel free to ask about this at every stage of your contact with the company: most people will be happy to tell you. But remember, what they say the process is, and what it *really* is, may be rather different!

Another way of finding out what the process is, is to phone up the personnel department, or the department who may hire your services, and ask someone (preferably someone lower down) who is in charge of hiring services like yours.

If in doubt, aim your pitch at the top because they will pass it down to the right person. They may take a personal interest. They will definitely add stature to your proposal by handing it to their subordinate: that means it will achieve much more attention. The people at the top like to show who's boss at times and will ignore the procedure in special cases. Their staff will often stick rigidly to procedure to avoid any trouble since they have little incentive to deviate. Hence, when looking for a job, it is seldom worthwhile pitching to the personnel department. Go for the person who's going to be paying for your services from his/her budget, or his boss.

Try to appreciate the strength of personalities involved here. A phone call to an editor of an industry magazine or a chat to someone at the stand of an exhibition (especially of a competitor) will elicit information on the personality of the decision-maker. Or you could make a phone call to the company asking for information about a product and manoeuvre the conversation to the personalities involved.

Sometimes the decision-maker may not be whom you expect. And you may have to network with several key people in a large organisation to succeed.

Case study: who is the real decision-maker?
A classic marketing situation is that of the company which supplied medical disposables to hospitals. The sales manager was trying to persuade the purchasing department that his surgeon's medical gloves were cheaper and that he could deliver more promptly than the hospital's existing supplier. He was actually approaching a person of lower power in the process: in fact the surgeons had the greatest power in the hospital and, since these were surgeon's gloves, were very picky about the brand and much less susceptible to the price. He soon switched his priority efforts to the surgeons, while keeping the buyer fully persuaded.

Find connections and common interests with the potential 'work-giver'

If they don't know anything about you, you need to catch their interest pretty quickly. There are two kinds of connection you need to investigate:

- through mutual acquaintances; and
- through mutual areas of interest.

First, list all the areas in which you and the decision-maker are likely to have mutual interests or shared experiences, and then list all the possible mutual acquaintances. Then look for overlaps. Here are some suggestions for shared experiences:

- hobbies;
- industry;
- previous companies;
- live/lived in the same area;
- work/worked in the same area;
- sports interests;
- social interests;
- charity involvement;
- schools and education;
- training courses; and
- exhibitions attended.

You can usually get information about the interests of the decision-maker from press articles about the industry, 'Who's Who?' in the library, or from chats with editors and journalists, trade association officials, or customer-facing people from the target company. If you draw a blank, you will have to fall back on what few solid facts you have or explore possibilities of connections in your conversation with the decision-maker.

Find news about that person

Scan the trade magazines and local newspapers. Listen out for scraps of information about your contact. Consider going direct to the people who know the decision-maker such as the secretary or his boss. Useful information about which you can build a conversation could be:

- new baby;
- married;
- new contracts won;
- conference speech; and
- new promotion.

Find people connections

The second step, of finding people connections, is tougher, especially if you are new to the industry or the area. But effort here is critical because of the importance people place on recommendations and referrals from people they know. Take comfort from this saying:

> Wherever I go there's somebody I know.
> (And it gets better the older I get.)

Possible sources of information on connections of people could be:

- industry associations;
- professional associations (Chartered Institute of Marketing, Institute of Directors, etc);
- local associations; and
- previous employers.

One of the best ways of finding connections is to produce a 'mindmap', as shown in Figure 7.1. This will enable you to see

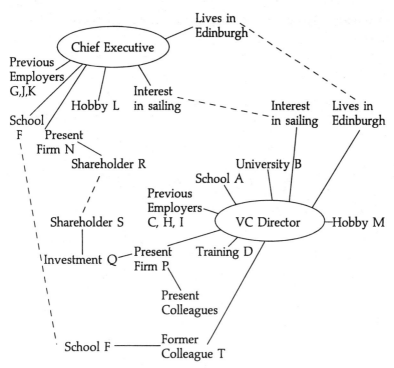

Figure 7.1 *Mindmap of people connections extended to include network partners*

gaps where we might be able to 'manufacture' connections. Journalists are expert at this. In the example shown here, the venture capital director wants to build a connection with the chief executive and the shareholders of a company in order to supply finance. At the top is the endpoint: the chief executive. At the bottom is the start point: the venture capital director. You can see that the two people live in the same city and enjoy sailing, connections with which a conversation could be opened. We will see in the next chapter how this mindmap can be extended to include network partners and their connections.

If in doubt, or you have very little information, then try making up an unusual connection which is likely to work. Consider: 'I happen to know someone who's a rally driver (same industry) who lives in Kent (where decision-maker works): maybe you know him?'

A real-life example of how these connections can be made to work is given below:

Case study
Michael once found a marketing job using a combination of skills. He had thought long and hard about his career options and had prioritised the industries he would like to work in. Third on the list was the motor industry. But he decided that he wanted to work for a smaller company to avoid bureaucracy.

Reading a report in a magazine he listed all the smaller companies. Then by chance he read a careers magazine which had a one-page interview with the managing director of one of them. So he made a copy of it and searched for more information. Reading a marketing magazine, he saw an article about the new marketing director who had been there six months (it is well known that managers like to restructure their departments within about six months of joining). A quick visit to a showroom and a chat with a sales manager there gave him the exposure to the products and the problems of the company. Then he wrote a letter to the Marketing Director, mentioning all the connections he had with the company and the industry, several paragraphs of his achievements in similar areas, and some knowledge of the company's problems. He won an interview and was able to win the job.

Summary

- Focus on what you want to achieve and how people can help you.
- Use your network partners and written sources to find suitable companies.
- Gather key information about these companies to understand their needs.
- Figure out who has the power to hire you and your services.
- Find people connections and areas of interest.

CHAPTER 8

How to Reach Targeted Individuals Through Your Network Partners

You can reach the decision-maker or network spider either directly or through a network partner. The most effective way to get the person to listen to you is through a referral or recommendation by a third party – your 'network partner'. There are two sub-strategies outlined here: having your network partner effect an introduction; and the longer-term strategy of having the network partner spread good word-of-mouth about you to the decision-maker.

How to choose the best network partner

Having worked out who is the key decision-maker or network spider you want to contact, you then need to work out how to get to him or her through your network partners. Extending the mindmap from the previous chapter to include people who can connect you with the 'work-giver' will make clear which of your network partners is likely to be the best person to help you.

In Figure 8.1, we see that the director of the venture capital company has found a few connections with the decision-maker:

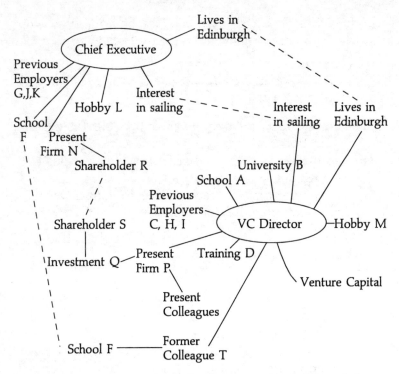

Figure 8.1 *Mindmap of people connections extended to include network partners*

- A former colleague of the venture capital director went to the same school as the chief executive of the target company.
- The shareholder of one of the venture capital firm's deals knows someone who invested in the target company.

How to persuade your network partner to help you

Don't forget why a network partner would want to help you (refer to Chapter 5 again). Most of these reasons will cost you little more than a beer but in some areas of business like venture capital where information on opportunities is a critical success factor, 'finder's fees' are offered for network partners who bring deals. Make sure you are clear in your mind why each person you contact would be happy to help you.

How to persuade your network partner to get you an introduction

In the example above, the venture capital director should ask for an introduction from one or other of the two people. This is quite normal practice. A degree of subtlety should be exercised about this, however.

And the venture capital director has two mutual interests with which he can open his conversation:

- The venture capital director lives in Edinburgh, as does the chief executive of the target company.
- Both enjoy sailing.

You need to think ahead and perhaps help your network partner with possible conversational openings.

How to build word-of-mouth with them about you and your services

Your network partners should not just be seen as scouts that you send out into the wilderness to reconnoitre the terrain, but also as troubadours and trumpeters who will broadcast tales of your brilliance. This is of course a longer-term and less certain method but the rewards can be significant. In some cases, there may realistically be no real way that the decision-maker will spare time for an introduction.

Conceive of the ideal scene: there is the person who has the 'Power', discussing with your network partner (or a contact of your network partner) that what he really needs is someone who can do X. And your contact gently releases to the person with power that he knows just the man (or woman), who can be reached on such and such a number.

Why is this so powerful an effect? It is because that people are so wary of hype nowadays, that the value of word-of-mouth and referrals has risen.

Just imagine the impact on a potential hirer of your services when he hears this second- or third-hand tale of your brilliance:

- He will tend to think that, because it usually takes something really special to get everyone talking about something, that you are worth paying attention to.
- Since you have not yourself broadcast the message, the fact that someone else is passing on that message without any possible benefit indicates it must be a true story, and worth listening to.
- Your story will gain stature from being told by your contact because he will trust your contact to pass on true information.

Summary

- Find the best network partner for your targeted individual.
- Persuade them to help you.
- Engineer an introduction if you can.
- Build word of mouth about yourself.

CHAPTER 9
How to Reach Targeted Individuals Directly

Now you have identified the person with the power to hire your services and what connections you can exploit, you need to know the mechanics of getting your message put in front of that person. The best way to get to someone who can hire you is through a word-of-mouth recommendation and introduction. This is not always possible and so here we outline the tactics of a direct approach to the person yourself.

After having read this chapter you should be able to select the best method for reaching the individual, working out how to get past the secretary, how to get the person to return your call, and understand the essentials of reaching him directly.

The next two stages are your opening conversational gambits and what to say after you say 'Hello'. These are dealt with in following chapters.

How to choose which direct approach to use

It is important to understand when to use the telephone and when to use a letter and a follow-up telephone call.

The telephone has many advantages and a few disadvantages:

- It is much more informal.

- It allows feedback.
- It is excellent for exploring possibilities in a non-threatening way.
- It requires much less effort to pick up the phone than to write a letter where every word may be scrutinised.
- Unfortunately, it requires openness and quick thinking on your part.
- It can be very difficult to find the person you want in his or her office.
- Some people find telephones very intrusive into their routine.

The letter also has advantages:

- It has the real advantage of providing a lot of information.
- It can be read at a convenient time by the recipient.
- It is better for shy people.
- It is a useful tool to get past the secretary.

Figure 9.1 shows the best suggested contact methods, depending on whether you know the person, have a connection or contact in common, and whether he/she is a potential source of information or a supplier of work. The letter on its own will almost never work for you and all letters must be followed up by a phone call. You should not expect the recipient to feel motivated to phone you unless your offer really is of immediate interest and is different from all the other approaches he will get.

Key points to note:

- Use the telephone for people you know, and who know you.
- Start with a letter for people who don't know you or anything about you.
- When phoning someone you know who is a potential work-giver, you may well want to follow up with a letter.

These are not hard and fast rules: sometimes you will want to remind your contacts about yourself with an outline CV and some notes on why you are good.

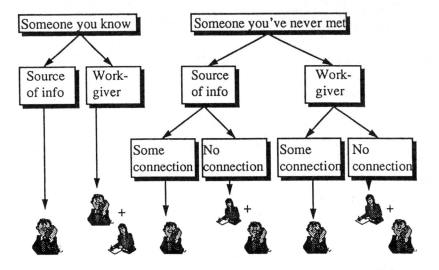

Figure 9.1 *Deciding which approach to use*

How to write letters that get results

Decide whether you are going to write a letter or not. If not, then skip to 'How to get past the secretary'. This section deals with crafting the all-important letter.

There are five stages to writing a contact letter:

- Establish your objective.
- Work out what their problems are.
- Devise three paragraphs which show you are the best person to solve these.
- Put them together in a linked and persuasive way.
- End in an action statement.

In most cases your objective should be to achieve an interview or a telephone discussion (which you should think of as the telephone equivalent of a meeting) from this letter, where you will build connections and get feedback.

Using the techniques of Chapter 3 and from mining all your contacts and press articles, you will have established the top three priorities for your targeted individual, and will have found examples in the past of your achievements. Therefore, what you must now do is put the two together. Write three short paragraphs where you outline in no more than two sentences one of your relevant achievements. Then end with a line like: 'And I'm sure I could help your company in the same way'. It is recommended that you prepare five or six paragraphs so that you only have to pull three from your list, making each letter much easier to write.

Start the letter in a friendly way which brings out your key connections in the first line if possible. This should act as a 'hook' to get the reader to read on to the interesting bits.

Do not write a humble scraping letter: you are an individual who has unique skills, experience and enthusiasm to offer. You are a supplier, not a slave. You have something useful to offer them that they should feel willing to pay the market price for.

End the letter with a two-line conclusion and the action statement that you will telephone them in three days' time to discuss their exact needs. Then don't forget to telephone them. If the person is not there try to get the secretary to register that you have phoned as promised. However, it is not recommended that you phone and leave a message more than four times: it becomes a waste of effort and appears undignified.

The important five elements can be seen in the two sample letters on pages 80 and 81.

How to get past the secretary

Most people will not stay at their desk much during their day, or they will be in meetings, or will not want to be disturbed. So you will need to get past the secretary or leave a message with the secretary.

Most people with the power to hire you will have a secretary. You must try hard to make the secretary your ally. However, they are rarely ambassadors for you. The secretary's role, among other things, is to act as a filter and an organiser of their manager's time.

Therefore the best way to get through to the decision-maker or network spider is to avoid the secretary altogether! If you phone early or late (say before 8.45 am and after 5.45 pm) you stand a very good chance of having the boss pick up the phone, before or after the secretary is at her desk, since most bosses work harder and longer hours than their teams.

Assuming you have not been able to get through out-of-hours, here are suggested lines which often work immediately in 30 per cent of calls:

- *'Is Jan in, please?'*
- *'I don't suppose Jan's in, is she?'*
- *'Jan Smythe, please.'*

If the secretary asks, 'What's it about?' you should recognise that this is the rock most people's vessel is stranded upon and answer strongly:

- *'I sent a letter and said I would call today.'*
- *'Michael Scrimshaw (an industry figure, a journalist) suggested I call her.'*
- *'We have a mutual friend who ...'*
- *'I was talking to Jan at the Widgets show and she asked me to call her.'*
- *'I was talking to David (the Managing Director) and he suggested Jan would be interested in ...'*

Don't forget to:

- sound professional;
- use first names where appropriate;
- act as though you have been good friends with the decision-maker for ages;
- appear to know everybody in the industry or company;
- act as if you have met the decision-maker;
- mention any special connection;
- act as though you fully *expect* her to put you through;
- don't sound weak;
- stand up to avoid squeezing your stomach;
- be friendly;

- smile: it really makes you sound more friendly;
- be calm; and
- show interest in the secretary and solving *her* problems.

You need therefore to charm the secretary and make sure you do not add to her tasks. If the person you want is not available, you must be polite and ask: 'If now is not convenient, when would be a good time to call?' See if you can book a time for, say, ten minutes as a telephone meeting and get the secretary to write it into the decision-maker's diary.

Since the person may be difficult to reach, may have more pressing engagements, have poor time-management skills and allow other meetings to run over your appointment, an alternative is to find a way to get that person to return your call when they have a free moment.

How to get them to return your call

Since few people will be motivated to return your call, you must try very hard to get through to the person yourself, or book a time. If all else fails, however, your only option before writing another letter or abandoning them is to get the decision-maker to return your call.

This requires very special skills. For you will have to leave a message with the secretary or on their office answering machine that is short, may be taken down wrongly, and must be very enticing to persuade the person to go to the trouble of picking up the phone.

Use the same ideas as above, but add a few twists:

- Say everything slowly.
- Always leave a contact number.
- Suggest a time when he or she can phone (and be available at that time).
- Puff up your title if possible: Product Manager is better than Product Planning Controller. Most of our titles are inaccurate and meaningless outside the organisation, anyway.
- Express urgency.

- Always push your connections.
- Avoid leaving details of your products or services.
- Don't make it sound like a sales call.

After you have overcome your natural shyness, with which the next chapter will help you, you will be learning the critical art of successful opening conversational gambits.

Summary

- Decide which direct approach to use.
- Figure out whether you should write a letter or not.
- If so, write persuasive letters about your achievements.
- Be able to demonstrate how your achievements show you can help them.
- Have a line ready to get past the secretary.
- Act as though you expect to be put through.
- Be ready to leave a short compact persuasive message for the decision-maker.

CHAPTER 10
Overcome Your Natural Shyness

Since using the telephone is a critical tool in networking and most people are nervous on the phone, we all need to overcome our natural shyness. In order to conquer any problem we first have to be aware of it, face it squarely and then be ready to act. The biggest problems are often ones of attitude.

Therefore, in this chapter, we will examine whether shyness is a difficulty for you, help you defeat your internal doubts and then build skills through practice in lower-risk areas.

Be aware of your natural inhibition

It is not easy, at first, for anyone to pick up the phone, to start talking, ask for information and eventually ask for help. But the first step in relieving oneself of anxiety is shining light on the difficulty. So ask yourself some questions to see if this is a problem for you:

	Yes	No
Do you feel nervous about the benefits of what you're offering?	☐	☐
Have you delayed picking up the telephone?	☐	☐

Does the prospect of talking to strangers fill you with trepidation?	☐	☐

If you ticked 'Yes' more than once, you should recognise that you have a natural mental block to overcome. Read the following few pages carefully and reinforce in your mind that only a little outward-going nature is needed and that this is necessary in order to achieve your objectives.

You're asking for information, not for work

Throughout the book we have emphasised that, in the main, you are only asking for information, not a job or work itself. What can be so difficult about asking for information, you should ask yourself? Imagine asking someone for directions, or what time the swimming pool closes. Here all you are doing is asking where opportunities might lie and could they perhaps let you know if other possibilities come up.

You're not threatening them

All you are asking for is information. They will not give you confidential information and you would not ask for it. You are not asking for work so they will not be threatened by feeling obliged.

Examine the range of their possible fears and how you should address them:

'He's going to ask me for work and I will feel obliged.'	No you aren't and he won't!
'I feel bad because I don't know anyone in this area.'	You will not push too hard or leave too many empty silences so that he will feel uncomfortable.
'If I can't help him, he might not help me in the future.'	You are cheerful and lively on the phone, with a smiling face. Everything is 'no

59

	problem' in your style and you leave plenty of room for him to be open.
'He is going to make me ask someone for a job and I might get rejected.'	You are not asking him for a job, or even for him to ask someone else about work. You are only asking for news of opportunities and ideas.
'If I recommend he sees Mr X what if he embarrasses me in front of Mr X with a poor job?'	You need to make clear to your contact that you are good and that you will not let him down.

Why they want to help you

It might amaze you to know that there really are people out there who genuinely enjoy being of help and will volunteer their time and effort on your behalf. You should enter into every networking conversation with the expectation that each one is just that sort of person, but with your being sensitive enough to spot when you're asking for too much. For further encouragement imagine yourself on the receiving end when a call comes through. Naturally, you would be helpful and flattered, wouldn't you?

Take a look at why people might want to help you and fortify yourself with the knowledge:

- Doing good makes them feel good.
- They know you or others will help them one day.
- Older people like to help the younger generation.
- They feel liked and flattered by your respect.
- They can imagine themselves in your position.
- They respect what you are doing.
- They admire people with your get-up-and-go.
- They want to be associated with winners like you.

How to make them like you

You are a nice person, aren't you? Aren't they going to enjoy catching up with news from you? Of course they are. A few other ideas you might use to make them like you are:

- Say thank you.
- Do them a little favour.
- Tell them something funny.
- Tell them something they didn't know which might interest them.
- Be honest and open.
- Give them news about mutual friends.

How to build your confidence with practice: the PIE method

The interview method recommended by all the careers counsellors is called PIE: for Pleasure, Information and Employment. There is no substitute for just getting on the telephone and calling. But here are ways of learning how to overcome natural shyness in a low-risk environment.

Make some calls and arrange some meetings with somebody who does something you find pleasurable and would enjoy talking about. For example, if you like fishing, go down to the river bank on a Sunday and talk to a stranger about fishing. Nothing formal, nothing heavy – just a chat. Get comfortable with going up to strangers and encouraging them to tell you more than you'll ever want to know. Remember what it feels like. You will soon be able to do the same with people who can help you to find work and jobs.

Then make some of the informational interviews recommended earlier in the book. Remember, you are just after information. Write down what they say and try to fill pages of your notebook. This will give you encouragement and help you to overcome your fear by keeping you busy.

When you really have become skilful then you can give the 'work-giver' decision-maker a call and not feel nervous about it. He or she admires you for contacting them and for not sitting on your behind. You clearly want work and have invested some effort in finding out about the company, its problems, that person and your connections. You are worth listening to, and meeting.

Use this method and you will soon overcome your natural shyness. If at any time you become nervous again, spend a little more time gathering information. This is a proven method. It has worked for others. It will work for you, too.

Self-marketing is the only answer

And finally, when you go to pick up the call for the first time, remember two things. First, that the first time is always the hardest, and second, that there is no alternative to a little self-marketing if you want to compete today.

Summary

- Be aware of your natural shyness.
- There is no need to feel shy about asking for information.
- Be careful to avoid appearing threatening.
- People like helping someone who asks for help.
- Make yourself likeable so they will like you.
- Practice makes perfect.
- Learn to interview for pleasure, information, then employment.
- They will never know you exist if you don't tell them.

CHAPTER 11
Opening Conversational Gambits

This chapter deals with the actual opening words you use when speaking to a decision-maker or potential network partner. By this time you have identified the person you wish to speak to and have thought about how they can help you and you them. You now need to make contact. So this is where you turn the theory into action. Most people feel very nervous at this stage yet the mechanics are relatively straightforward: you are good and they should want to hire your services. This chapter is designed to help you make the first step and get your foot in the door.

The very first words

Since the person on the other end of the telephone doesn't know you, your key objectives are to make him or her want to listen to you. You do this by making him like you (be cheerful), by being recommended (exploiting a connection), by having something interesting to talk about (a common interest), by having something of benefit to him (you have a silver bullet for his hot-button-need), or by making him respect you as an equal professional (following up on a letter).

Wear interview clothes

When first picking up the telephone it is a good idea to dress up in formal work clothes as if going to an interview so that you act professionally.

Stand up as if being introduced face to face

This has the effect of putting you in the right mind-set as well avoiding 'scrunching' up your stomach, so improving your delivery and making you sound much more confident. Take several deep breaths before picking up the telephone.

Start with a cheery voice

- 'Good morning!'
- 'Hello there, my name is ...'

Act casually and friendly

- Use first names when mentioning people you have met (but stay formal for the new contact).
- Use conversational language to put the contact at ease and depressurise the situation.
- Use 'I'm' rather than 'I am'.

If necessary, clarify that the person you are speaking to is the right person

There are few things more embarrassing than getting your key sentences out and finding that you have just spoken to the wrong person!

- 'Good morning is that Mr ...? Hello there, ...'
- 'Hello, I'm looking for Mr ... Can you help?'

Always begin with your name upfront

This makes you appear honest, open and *bona fide*. Your company, where appropriate, should be used as well. If you are looking for a job this is not advised. However, if the recipient does not know of your company try to avoid getting him distracted by telling him what the company does until later.

- *'My name is ... and I'm telephoning to ...'*
- *'It's Tom Vermassen here from Human Products Inc. ... and I was wondering ...'*

Think of yourself as being on the same level as your contact

You are not on the scrounge. You have a service or product to offer which you are proud of. It is honourable to offer such services for sale – you should not need to bow and scrape. Therefore, don't use terms such as 'sir' or 'madam'.

Act confidently

Go into the conversation fully expecting the contact to want to take you and your services on if he is able to. You should act as though there are lots of other people in the wings willing to buy this product, yet you would very much like this contact to be on board.

Be short and to the point

- *'I'm telephoning to ...'*

Allow the other an escape route

Remember that the person doesn't know you at all, and is likely to be busy. Some people appreciate diversions from outside, some people are just too stretched. Try to be sensitive to these aspects. Note that standard sales techniques advise never leaving the other person a chance to say 'no' but people have become very wise to this over the last half-century and you will find that this polite approach goes a long way.

- *'Is now a good time?'*
- *'Would you be able to spare a few minutes?'*
- *'If now is not convenient, when would be a better time to call?'*
- *'Are you in a meeting? Should I call later?'*

How to make your contact want to hear more

Exploit your connections

- *'Good morning, ... Fred Potter suggested I call.'*
- *'I was talking to Bill Good at the ... Conference and he said you might be able to help me/give me some advice/appreciate a call/ need a plumber ...'*

Provide the silver bullet for his hot-button need

You have heard on the grapevine that he has a need you can fill. Try not to be too blunt in case you come across as presumptuous, arrogant or plain wrong! Go in obliquely, be ready to back off, explain where you got the information from, and leave sentences open to allow a smoother end.

- *'I understand from Bill Woodside that you might be looking for a person who can help you in the area of ...'*

Follow up on a letter

Since following up on a letter is much easier than phoning an unknown person out of the blue, it is always a good idea to send a letter first. That way you have a ready-made entry and they know quite a lot about you already, which means they will start to mention common interests and connections.

- *'I'm calling you to ask whether you received the letter I sent you two days ago'.* If your contact hasn't seen your letter, explain why you are calling and then offer to re-send the letter, saying you will telephone again after he has received it.
- *'I sent you a letter the other day and wondered when we should get together to discuss it.'*
- *'I sent you a letter and wondered if you had had time to read it.'*

Bring up common interests in your conversation

Generally, it can be difficult to bring up common interests in the first sentence unless that is the reason you are calling.

- *'I noticed an interesting article in the ... newspaper and thought it might be of interest to you and your business. Have you had time to read it?'*

66

Follow up on some news about the contact

- *'Congratulations on your new baby. How is your partner?'*
- *'I hear that you won the ... contract. Congratulations.'*
- *'I see that from the local paper that you are expanding at a fast rate and I thought that perhaps ...'*

Employ a little flattery

Depending on the person and the mood they are in, they will respond positively to respect and, if done with a light, perhaps humorous, touch, to flattery. Consider being blatant and outrageous, too.

- *'I understand that after your recent promotion to Manager of European Sales, that you are now in charge of half the planet. So I expect you would be interested in ...'*
- *'My industry contacts all mention XYZ company as being one of the top companies in the productivity stakes and ...'*

Always connect your sentences to an action or question

This allows you to move on from our opening phrases to the meat of the discussion without ending up with painful empty spaces.

- *'... and I feel that ...'*
- *'... so you probably ...'*
- *'... therefore I expect that you ...'*

Measure interest and build commitment

- Allow the other time to say something.
- Wait for a response.
- Try to be sensitive to whether they are receptive.
- When trying to build commitment ask phrases in a way to make them say yes:
  - —*'Does this sound of interest to you?'*
  - —*'Increasing profits through increased productivity is something most companies think about in recession, wouldn't you agree?'*

Putting it all together

The most successful opening combines the above phrases. Here are some examples. It helps to write out your first few sentences before you phone so that you can overcome your nervousness and make it sound very slick.

> *'Good morning, I'm looking for Mr Burwood ... Hello, there, it's John Doakes from Jones & Harpie. I happened to be talking to John Heywood the other day. I understand you know John Heywood from the Sailing Club? [wait for response] Well, he suggested I give you a call to see whether you know anyone who ...'*

> *'Hello, Mr Burridge, my name's Jim Hale. We haven't met before but I noticed your promotion in the trade magazine last month; congratulations on your new appointment [wait for response]. I thought I'd give you a call now that you have your feet under the table to introduce myself and I wondered whether we might meet .... When would be a good time?'*

> *'Good morning, I'm Geoff Dodge and I'm calling you about a letter I sent you two days ago about ... Do you remember receiving it? OK, allow me to recap quickly. Is now a good time? Can you spare me a minute? Fine. The letter explained how my services might well be of use in ...'*

Summary

- Be cheerful.
- Be confident.
- Be upfront and to the point.
- Exploit connections as recommendations.
- Mention common interests.
- Mention news.
- Wait for a response.
- Write down your opening lines before picking up the phone.

CHAPTER 12

What to Say After You've Said 'Hello'

Having opened the conversation you need to direct it towards the two critical stages of gathering information and getting the names of the next level of contacts. We investigate tricky issues about handling meetings and lunches, and when to ask for work directly (and when not to!). You will find these approaches of use for speaking to both your network partners and the decision-makers.

Deciding whether to use the phone, a meeting or lunch

In most cases you will want to spend more than a few minutes on the telephone to get more time with the contact. A telephone conversation should therefore be limited to the following circumstances:

- when you have very little time;
- when you feel the contact is likely to be of limited use;
- when you already know the person well and have met them lately; and
- when the contact is located far away.

In all other cases a meeting or a lunch appointment is

recommended. A longer time together has several key advantages:

- It gives the contact another opportunity to think about the next level of contacts.
- If you have never met them before this meeting will fix you in their minds – which is useful if they hear of anything in the future.
- If they are very well connected you will need time for all this to come out.
- It will give you a general overview.
- If you want to recruit them as an ongoing network partner they will need to know a lot about you and will need to be persuaded that you are *bona fide*.
- You are showing them respect by going to visit them.

It is usually best to go to see them in their office: most people are busy but are happier to use company time to see you than their personal time.

Choosing between a meeting and a lunch is relatively easy. Lunches and drinks are what you offer someone you know already, or someone who is already responding well to you. Do not attempt to press a lunch (especially an expensive sit-down restaurant meal) on anyone you do not know well: they may well see this as an obligation on them. Besides which it is likely to be expensive and not cost- or time-efficient.

If your contact takes you out for lunch then expect to pay your half, which reinforces that you are equals.

The informational interview

Of course, you are looking for opportunities for your services and products, but recognise that even this contact may very well not be able to offer you anything. Therefore the key objective of this informational interview is to find out information on where you might look for opportunities and who you might talk to about them.

This mind-set is critical in overcoming the beginner's fear of going to meet someone. It is also very important that this is fully and explicitly communicated to your contact. Otherwise he will feel under an obligation and will feel very uncomfortable. If your contact says, 'I can't offer you work, sorry. Therefore I have no time to see you', you must realise that you have not sold this meeting right. Explain that it is really only information and advice you are after and ask when would be convenient for you to come and see him.

How should you structure your questions? Some useful frameworks for remembering questions are:

- 3Cs: Company, Customers, Competitors
- 5Ps: Prices, Products, Positioning, Promotion, Place (= Distribution)

Some suggested questions are:

- Who are the customers?
- Are they changing?
- Who is the competition?
- What is happening with the competition?
- Where do most people make money in this business?
- What is happening in his company?
- What are the forces on the players in this industry and how are they changing the industry?
- What are the new products or services in the industry?
- Where are the growth areas?
- What are the trends in the costs of supplies?

You need to understand the important rules of active listening in order to extract the maximum amount of information and make the network partner feel good about you:

- Say 'Uh-huh', 'OK', 'Oh, I see' often.
- Ask questions of clarification.
- Ask what something means to him.
- Repeat what he says with a question to extract more information:

  Contact: *'Costs are increasing.'*
  You: *'Costs are increasing, then? Tell me more.'*
  Contact: *'We have to find ways to do things more cheaply ...'*

To avoid this being a one-way affair, do some research beforehand and inject some interesting snippets of information into the conversation:

- *'I saw an interesting article about that the other day.'*
- *'I heard that Fred Squick was promoted to . . .'*
- *'Is that related to the decline in market share reported in the trade magazine?'*

After you have asked for names of other people to provide you with more information (see below), don't forget to ask whether he is happy for you to phone him in the future if you have any further queries (this keeps up an ongoing dialogue and keeps the channels open). And leave your card (business card or personal card) saying that if he hears anything you would be very grateful for any more information and this is how he can reach you.

Finding the next stage of network partners

Perhaps the most important objective of any contact, at least initially when you are still quite a way from your decision-maker, is to find out the names and telephone numbers of the next stage of network partners. Don't let your contact go without getting at least three names from him. This will be difficult to do at first: you will have to be comfortable with silence as he racks his brains for names. Don't fill in the silence and let him off the hook!

As you can see in Figure 12.1, this will massively expand the number of listening posts and sources of information.

In just four stages, your initial contact has led you to 39 new network partners.

Don't forget to ask your contact whether he is happy for you to mention his name with any of these contacts. In most cases there will be no objections. This will greatly increase your chances of getting through the secretaries and their natural reticence to speak to an unknown.

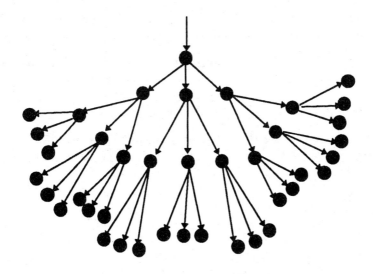

Figure 12.1 *Networking is like a chain reaction*

How and when to ask for work directly

In most cases the rule of thumb should be not to ask for work directly. People usually bridle at this. This is particularly true when looking for employment. Be oblique and subtle at all times.

If you are looking for employment and the contact offers you a job, beware! This is a well-known trap and how you handle this may dictate whether you blow the whole shebang. If offered a job, then say that you are flattered and that you are conducting a survey of the industry/area and when you have finished you will be in a better position to evaluate which of the opportunities available are best for you. Say this without appearing arrogant, but make it understood that you are just looking for information at this stage.

There are a few occasions when you should ask for work, however:

- when you are getting very strong buying signals; and
- when the decision-maker is asking about incidental details

73

like delivery or contractual guarantees, or is telling you about specific opportunities in his firm.

If in doubt, always ask indirectly. And try to do this casually (perhaps with a smile). Avoid finding yourself trying to convince him that you are the right person. Use questions rather than statements.

- *'So do you think there may be opportunities in the future?'*
- *'Do you think this may be something I could help you with?'*

Summary

- Decide how to get more time with your contact.
- Build your mind-set around asking for information and further contact names, not work at this stage.
- Prepare a list of questions to ask.
- Gather information and explore the possibility of opportunities for your services.
- Get at least three other names of people to talk to.
- Avoid asking for work directly, unless the situation is very clear.

CHAPTER 13

Overcome Your Fear of Rejection

Now that you have overcome your blocks in picking up the phone and speaking to a stranger, you may still have to conquer the other natural fear of rejection. This chapter will help you to prepare for not always having things your way every time.

You're offering them something useful

By offering your services, either as a supplier or as an employee, you are making a contribution to society, as someone who will provide what the customer wants at a price that they find gives them value. You pay taxes to society and, by earning money, do not rely on other taxpayers to support your standard of living. You should have no guilt or qualms about what you are doing.

They're not rejecting you

If a 'work-giver' should choose not to take up your proposal, then he or she is not rejecting you, only your proposal. Make sure you understand this important distinction and be careful not to take these minor setbacks personally. Try to understand the possible reasons for the rejection of your proposition, adapt your offering, and come to terms with them:

- No budget right now.
- Needs fully covered at the moment.
- Can't see any benefit of your offering compared to existing supplier.
- Doesn't want to take the risk to change to you.
- You're too expensive.
- Doesn't understand your offering.
- You're good but someone he knew better made the same offer.

You have been successful in the past and will be again

You are good at what you do. You have had substantial achievements in the past. If the 'work-giver' chooses not to take you up on your offer, more fool him for missing out on a real opportunity.

To fortify yourself, note down your major achievements in this area and which make you able to prove you are good at this activity:

-
-
-
-
-
-

Why every 'no' takes you nearer a 'yes'

To some extent, all of this self-marketing business is a 'numbers game':

- In direct marketing through the mail, marketers regard themselves as very successful if they get over 2 per cent response.
- In selling advertising space in a certain magazine over the telephone, most salespeople will sell one page every week. If they make 50 calls a day that means on average they have to go through 249 noes to get to a 'yes'.

You need to realise that not everybody out there will want what you have to offer. So welcome the noes because the more you have under your belt, the nearer you are to a 'yes'. Even if it didn't work out this time, it will work the next time, or the time after that if you don't give up.

Make a list of where you didn't do something the first time but went on to achieve it, or went around it, or where not reaching your goal never mattered in the end (eg your driving test, your school exams).

-
-
-
-
-

Plenty of fish in the sea

Steel yourself by reminding yourself that there are in fact many companies who can provide you with work and opportunities. Don't let any one company, however seemingly unique, make you obsessed. 'When you can't get the job you want, go for the nearest thing'.

What you are doing is brave, adventurous and entrepreneurial

You are a hero in picking up the telephone. You are not willing to sit there and let life pass you by. You are 'getting on your bike'. You are answering the pioneer's call to have the right to determine his own future and build his freedom. Would a hero collapse if he tripped over the first hurdle?

Nothing good was ever won easily

We never said it was going to be easy, though after a little practice you shouldn't find it too difficult. It is worth all the trouble. And there is no alternative. Like a guy wanting to meet a pretty girl, who has to walk across a lonely empty dance floor and risk rejection, you too have to risk rejection to get what you want.

If you don't ask, you don't get

And finally, ask yourself what is the most you can lose from trying. No one was ever ridiculed for trying to make a better life, or earn more money. The effort you are expending is not expensive, nor very time consuming (if you are focused and really care about your objective). You have nothing to lose but your chains.

Summary

- What you are offering will be perceived as useful.
- Rejection is not an indication of your worth.
- Everybody has their little setbacks.
- Every 'yes' has to be won by accepting a few noes.
- There are always other options.
- Think of this hunt as an adventure.
- If it was so easy everybody would have done it before you.
- How do they know you want something if you don't ask?

CHAPTER 14
Follow-up Tactics

So you've made contact, either with the key decision-maker or with an intermediate contact, now what? Follow-up becomes critical in ensuring continuing attention by the contact, in gaining more information, and in winning yourself more quality time to present your proposal.

In this chapter we deal with follow-up letters and how to ensure a steady flow of information by giving feedback to your network partners.

The thank-you letter

A good rule of thumb is that you should send a thank-you letter, or some sort of follow-up letter, to most people you meet for several reasons:

- It is well known that people keep in their mind people they have met most recently.
- Sending a letter requires some effort, which is recognised by the recipient as showing you care about him or her.

Where would you use a letter? When you have talked to a contact about looking out for opportunities for you, it is important to:

- thank them for their time;
- remind them of what you can offer a 'work-giver';

- give them a note of anything you said you would do for the contact;
- leave an opportunity for them to ask you if there is anything you can do for them.

When you have asked someone for information about an industry, a company, or a person, don't forget a thank-you note with a contact number, saying how grateful you would be if they come across anything new that might help you.

Particularly important is a message to a key decision-maker. They have spared time to see you. Remember that this letter will very probably go on file, and will act as your ambassador when your file is passed to a secondary decision-maker.

Don't forget also to send letters to people you have just met (either likely information sources or decision-makers) with whom you would like to stay in contact. This is often surprisingly overlooked by even the most systematic networkers. Make clear that you enjoyed meeting them and why. Remind them who you are. Mention areas of common interest and suggest ways you could be of use to the recipient. End with an action point, such as you will call them by a certain time. Be wary of mentioning a specific need at the moment, unless you are able to subtly drop it in as a 'by the way' line at the end. If you do this, don't expect the contact to pick up the telephone to you: you have to make the running.

Here are two sample letters, the first for finding contracts, the second for finding jobs.

Dear Mr X

Thank you for the time you spared me yesterday. I very much appreciated your help in providing me with some leads I can follow up. I will let you know how things progress.

Just to recap, my company has been supplying garden furniture hand-made from Douglas Pine to traditional New England styling for several years. Our strengths are our unique styling, our quality of finish and our reliable delivery. I am sure

---

that clients who really appreciate the good things in life will be just as satisfied as our existing clients.

Highlights of the company's achievements are:

- winning the Gold Prize at the Covent Garden furniture festival in 1993;
- selling 1,500 items per year to the Japanese;
- described by *House & Gardening Furniture* magazine as 'the very finest garden furniture money can buy'.

As promised, Mr X, our company's product literature is enclosed. If, after reviewing it, any further suggestions as to potential clients come to mind, I would be very grateful if you could let me know.

Thank you again for your help. I will keep you up to date on progress and look forward to talking to you soon.

Yours sincerely

Dear Mr X

Thank you for the time you spared me yesterday. I very much appreciated your help in providing me with some leads I can follow up. I will let you know how things progress.

Just to recap, I am a marketing manager experienced in key account liaison, setting up distribution channels, and customer service. My strengths are in understanding and exceeding customer needs in this industry. I feel that these skills would also be able to make a substantial contribution to a company with a high brand awareness who wishes to increase its level of customer service.

My most significant achievements have been:

- increasing sales of key accounts in my region by 32 per cent over two years by cross-selling of products;

- Manager in charge of setting up a chain of 89 retail outlets over a period of two years, all reaching above-average profitability within one year of start-up;
- Moving the company division from tenth in national rankings to second in customer service within one year, by developing new products with customers, installing computer systems to reduce lead-time, and remotivating the customer-facing team.

My CV, as promised, is enclosed. If, after reviewing it, other names of suitable companies or search firms come to mind, I should be very grateful if you would let me know.

Thank you again for your help. I will keep you up to date on progress and look forward to talking to you soon.

Yours sincerely

Feedback to your original contact

It is really critical to keep your network partners informed how your search is going on, particularly with respect to the network partners they have given you. It is polite and if nothing else will bring your name back into the front of their mind.

To save time, and to encourage more ideas from your contact, I recommend that you use the telephone. By now it should be easy to pick up the conversation where you left it.

'Hello, it's ... and I'm just calling to say hello and to update you on progress in my search for ... [wait for response] First of all, thanks again for the names you gave me when I last called. I called Mr Y and he was able to tell me about opportunities in a growing area in his sector, and gave me three names of people I can talk to there. I don't suppose you know of anybody in that area, do you?'

Imagine how that contact must feel now. You have involved

him in your quest and you are showing appreciation and respect. Who would not respond favourably:

'Yes, you should call Sam Shepard at XYZ Technologies. I've heard they're growing and I read somewhere that they are teaming up with CDG Medical to make an electronic deep-vein thrombosis device. Your skills could be very useful there I should think. Why not give him a call?'

'That reminds me. I was thinking about what you provide the other day when I was talking to Bill at Hepway Inc and I mentioned your name to him. You should give him a call.'

Summary

- Use the thank-you letter for your scouts, for information-providers, for decision-makers, and people you would like to know better.
- Remind them of your achievements.
- Keep your network partners informed about progress on the leads they have given you.

CHAPTER 15

Build Your Visibility with Personal PR

This is the third major networking technique. It is longer term than the others, requires continued concerted effort but the pay-off is that the effects can be very significant and endure for a long time.

Once you have clear in your mind whom you want to receive your message, you need to select a stage on which to perform. Remember that the key is to become memorable so that people will not forget you.

We begin with relatively elaborate networking outside your company, making sure they remember your name and move on to building visibility within your company and remembering their name.

Choose the audience

Your audience should be the decision-makers and network partners on whom you will rely for help in giving you contracts and jobs, in passing on information about those opportunities to you, in introducing you to decision-makers, and spreading good word-of-mouth about you.

So go back to the objective and target sector you defined for yourself in Chapter 3 and the ideas you developed on who the decision-maker is (in Chapter 7).

Choose the 'stage'

Shakespeare said that all the world's a stage, and all the men and women merely players upon that stage: think of all the ways of getting to those players you can, then prioritise the most cost- and time-effective. Imagine yourself as a public relations executive trying to raise the profile of the product that is you. How can you persuade the media or the decision-makers and network partners themselves to take an interest in you? Think of something different to achieve 'cut-through'.

We start with the more high-profile ideas and then develop easier ways to start building visibility without really trying.

Build a reputation as an industry expert

Become the person everyone talks about and asks for an opinion. Become the Kissinger of your industry. How do you do it if you don't have years in the industry?

- Write articles in the industry magazine. What is the magazine they all read? Can you become featured in it as a news item? Who would you need to charm? How could you do it?
- Prepare a research report on a subject of great interest and send it out free to decision-makers

Get through to decision-makers at times when they are concentrated together

If, for example, you feel that the best buyers for your computer credit-risk software program are credit controllers in smaller companies in the suburbs of London then you need to find a venue where they are all going to get together. Is there an association of credit controllers which has a Christmas party? If so, why not take out half a page of advertising in the menu? Or place a stand outside the venue. Or sponsor a raffle prize. Or make a donation to the favourite charity on the night.

Questions you need to ask yourself for all your ideas are:

- What do you want to feel associated with?
- When are they going to be most receptive?
- Where can your best strengths be used?
- Who do you know who can help you build visibility with your target sector?

Eight successful techniques for building your visibility

Here are some additional possible stages on which to perform:

Enter an industry competition

In architecture young talent is often spotted by their entering national competitions to design an imaginary building. Does something like this exist in your industry? Can you organise one?

Enter your company into a float competition

Companies which want to build their profile in the local community often take part in float competitions: they hire a truck and dress it up with coloured paper and drive in procession through the town during a festival. You could do the same.

Take exhibition space or hold your own show

You're talented and you have a portfolio of your work. Arrange a show and invite people to attend. This needn't be expensive nor time-consuming. If you can come up with something attractive to the public, your local library may be happy to set aside space for something unusual. If not, why not hire an area?

Take advertising space to say 'Well done for 50 years'

Companies often try to raise their profile among attendees of shows, plays and country events by taking out half a page in a programme. They tend to make them a little more subtle by expressing their congratulations on 'another year's show'. You could do the same.

Advertise in a low-profile way
Larger companies advertise their achievements of a deal done by placing advertisements in the paper notifying the completion of a deal. These are called 'tombstones'. Could you adapt this idea to work for you?

Perform charity and humanitarian work
Probably one of the most useful networking activities is to raise your profile by organising a fund-raising drive. Join Rotary, Round Table, or the Lions. Start your own charity!

Volunteer your services
You could donate your services, or those of the company, to doing good for free. Community services are often under-funded and are grateful for help. Help the local enterprise centre, pull pints behind the local theatre bar.

Take part in local activities
Do you feel strongly enough about something to want to take an active part? You are very likely to meet some interesting people and the project may be newsworthy enough for the media to follow.

Produce a newsletter
Why not produce a newsletter with news of the latest happenings in the area, in your company or the industry?

How to be visible without really trying

Not all visibility-raising methods require as much effort. There are myriad ideas you can easily use to raise your profile. Remember, most people are happy to slink in the shadows yet wonder why good opportunities never find them.

Try some of these out:

- Ask a question at a conference.
- Make a point in a meeting.
- Write letters to the letters page of the industry magazine.

- Introduce yourself to lots of people at an industry show or ball.
- Buy people a drink at the bar at a lecture.
- Discuss a book with an industry leader.
- Wear bright ties.
- Tell jokes.
- Have and express an opinion on everything (but recognise your limitations and keep an open mind!).
- Give out an unusual business card.
- Recast your CV to be a little different.
- Take up and talk about unusual (not too unusual!) hobbies and interests.

Make sure *they* remember *your* name

Your name is your address: if they like what you do but can't find you, you have achieved nothing. So it is very important to make people remember your name. Here are some hints:

Introduce yourself to others at every possible opportunity
This takes some doing at first if you are a little shy. Speak to people wherever you meet them: at parties, at work at the coffee machine, at conferences, in meetings, in the plane.

Ask them about themselves
Everybody has at least one interesting story to tell. And remember that conversations = connections. Try to find at least one person and activity you have in common.

Make sure the other person gets your name right
Spell it out for them if it could be unclear.

Give them your card if possible
So that they can remind themselves. It has your address and, most important, your telephone number, too.

Drop them a note or call them up afterwards
This follow-up activity helps to seal your name in their mind,

allows you to arrange to see them again and thereby helps you to reinforce the connection.

Build visibility at work

Work is a key place to raise your profile but presents a few difficulties: in most countries it can appear unseemly to market yourself too aggressively. Here are some ideas for you.

Do a good job
Straightforward and obvious, but sometimes mistakenly neglected by people who reckon that what you know is irrelevant compared to whom you know!

- Meet your promises.
- Exceed expectations: go the extra inch, if not the extra mile.
- Beat the budget.
- Beat the deadline.
- Produce better quality than expected.

Make sure people know you are doing a good job
If nobody knows you are working late and getting good results then how can you expect to be rewarded? You have to make sure the people who count know how well you are doing.

- Get your acquaintances to mention you in front of your boss.
- Ask people you are helping to mention your name.
- Give your boss notes of your achievements over the last six months so that or she can incorporate these in your performance review.

Stand out without appearing arrogant
Here are a few suggestions:

- Volunteer your time.
- Develop a reputation as a person for whom 'nothing is too difficult' (but strike a balance to avoid being exploited).

- Give full credit to other people's ideas you have incorporated in your work.
- Thank people publicly for their efforts in helping you.

Make sure *you* remember *their* name

One of the best ways of building a relationship with somebody is remembering their name the next time you meet, and where you last met. People like to be remembered.

Have you ever walked past somebody and then, recognising them from a long time ago, turned around and looked back only to find them looking at you. Then, when you talk to them they shake your hand and say out your name and start a conversation about a subject important to you as if you had seen each other just the other day?

They use the following well-known technique. Remembering someone's name is one of the best ways of showing that you care about them, and therefore of strengthening your relationship with them. It starts off by feeling a little unnatural, but it will soon become instinctive. Soon you will start noticing other people using the technique to remember your name!

The aim of the exercise is to associate their name (and later any of their interests) with their face. Think of trying to produce a police 'mugshot' where the name is held in front of the face. A famous piece of research showed that we learn and recall much better when we use several senses at the same time: so the idea is to excite your visual memory of faces, your visual memory of words, your hearing, and your memory of saying their name.

Here is how it works:

- As you shake hands with someone new, say their name out loud.
- As you say it, look hard at their face and try to fix it in your memory.
- See their face with their name written underneath.
- Hear your voice saying their name.
- Feel your lips producing the sounds.

If their name is unusual, ask them how they spell it. People feel flattered if you care enough to ask this; they feel offended if you write a letter to them with the wrong spelling, and it helps to put the name in concrete. It is also good manners!

Learn how to pronounce it the way they do: practise it with them while they are in front of you. If possible, write their name down in front of them and try to get their address and telephone number, too. Ask them for their card.

Try out the method a few times. At the end of the day you should be able to recall people's faces and then along will come the name and interest attached to the image.

Summary

- Decide to whom you would like to be more visible.
- Decide on which stage you are going to be more visible.
- Being able to remember somebody's name is important.
- Follow the eight successful techniques.
- Adopt the methods of being more visible without seeming to try.
- Find a way to stick in their memory.
- Don't neglect building visibility where you work.

CHAPTER 16
Maximise Your Networking Efforts

The skills you have picked up from this book so far can make you a better networker than almost anyone you will meet. Most people underestimate the power of networking, are thwarted by the psychological hurdles, and are not willing to be at all systematic. This book should have overcome these problems for you.

This chapter suggests possible avenues for further development to make you truly world class. Here are ways of being more popular, indexing your information better, and using modern networks like e-mail and Internet. You will by now have found that this is a life skill you can use all the time and we suggest other possible applications.

Become (even!) more likeable

The key to networking is to be the sort of person everyone wants to be in touch with. In other words, you become the 'friendly network spider'. Think about what characteristics these people have and you will instinctively (I hope) recognise Lyndon Johnson's guidelines from pages 26 and 27.

Be comfortable to be with and do not ask more of people than you yourself give. But the most crucial attitude is to respect every person as a unique individual. Everyone has a story to tell.

Everyone has at least one fascinating detail about them. Try to find out what it is. Ultimately this quote sums it up well:

'Everyone I meet has something to teach me. And, in that respect I will learn from him.'

Ralph Waldo Emerson

When you find yourself in this frame of mind, you will never allow yourself or other people to see networking as 'using' people.

Index your contact information

When you get into the swing of networking, you will find that you can easily generate three or four contacts or network partners from most gatherings you go to. Soon you will start to forget names and details and the usefulness of meeting these people will diminish. So it becomes a good idea to write down and organise your information. These details are crucial in maintaining a relationship, in helping them, and in being able to understand which person can help you solve a problem.

A glorified address book, or a personal organiser, are possible starts. A collection of business cards won't be enough on its own: you need to add notes about where you met them and some of their interests.

Perhaps the best technique is to get a box of 3' × 5' cards and organise them alphabetically and/or by subject for each person. Then you can stick on their business card (which saves having to rewrite details) and still have room for more details such as:

- names of partner and children
- telephone numbers
- home address
- birthdays of contact, children, wife
- St Patrick's Day, Oxford and Cambridge Boat Race day, an anniversary (or other day of interest to them)
- hobbies and sports

- where you met them
- whom else they know
- what they have done in the past
- what they look like (perhaps)
- any needs they have that you might be able to help them with one day

Birthdays of children, for example, you can usually obtain when they send out birthday announcements (if you are a friend). Or, don't be shy: phone them up and ask them!

Electronic address books are very useful, are much more portable, and have calendars which can remind you to telephone on certain days. They also have the big advantage of recovery of information when you lose your address book. With a paper diary you have to photocopy all the pages at regular intervals (not easy). With some of the electronic versions you can 'back up' your names and phone numbers on to your personal computer. Then it is easy to pull up the data. An investment worth considering.

Using electronic mail and the Internet

Many companies and individuals now have electronic postboxes to which you can send messages and from which they can access what you send them. These have great advantages for building and maintaining relationships, particularly where you have met face-to-face before.

Internet and the 'World-Wide Web' are becoming more important and now you can find people with similar interests all around the world. They subscribe to special interest 'bulletin boards' (such as on sailing) where people can converse via computer on any subject. If you wanted to find someone with connections in a certain area or industry you can place your request on an appropriate 'bulletin board'.

A life skill you can use all the time

When you follow the guidelines and techniques in this book you will become adept at networking in all spheres of your life. Networking, at its most basic, is information flow, about opportunities and about people:

- for finding finance;
- for finding supporters of a cause;
- for finding a source of supply;
- for getting an unbiased opinion on a product or service.

Summary

- Desire to be so likeable that you become naturally likeable.
- Contact information is like a garden and needs nurturing.
- Don't overlook the modern electronic communication methods.
- Networking is truly a skill which will affect your whole life.

CHAPTER 17
Action Steps Now

If you want what is rightfully yours in life you can't just wait for the phone to ring. You have to pick it up and dial.

In today's competitive world the only effective way of hearing about opportunities and standing out is through networking. Use it to:

- get your network partners to hear about opportunities for you;
- reach targeted individuals; and
- build visibility

Therefore, you need to:

- define your objective;
- work out your positioning;
- choose your best networking method;
- overcome your inhibitions; and
- pick up the telephone!

Just do it! Nike™